Naked

Ka hunaka'ii ola: kohana

MICHAEL LEMES

Cover and interior layout by Blue Pen

ISBN: 979-8-9858486-1-8 (paperback)
ISBN: 979-8-9858486-2-5 (ebook)

This book is dedicated to my children, Vraunwyn and Sorin, who are the greatest gifts in my life! They make my life richer every day.

Acknowledgements

The writings were never written for public view. These are intimate poems jotted down that started as a coping mechanism for stressful life events, further evolving into an expression of my life's path, giving it a voice that enabled me to grow and heal.

I have been motivated by a spiritual whisper to gift these works to my children with the purpose of uplifting them and others who are struggling through life's challenges, for them to know that they are not alone in this world. To inspire readers to find the inner strength, resilience, and perseverance to find their bright spot every day.

I would like to express my profound thanks to Victoria Griffin of Blue Pen. Without her assistance this book would have never come to be.

CONTENTS

Looking Glass

Awakening	3
Bleeding	4
Bloodsong	5
Caged	6
Half-Breed	7
Ekolu	8
Hand Glass	9
Ho'oponopono	10
Iron Sanctuary	11
Leo	12
Little Faith	13
Lost	14
Memory	15
Feral Child	16
Roar of the Surf	17
Rousing	18
The Angels Cried	19
Twilight	20

Love

Allure	23
Bliss	24
Breathtaking	25
Broken Solitude	26
Burning	27
Butterfly Kisses	28

Double-Edged Blade   29
Dreams   30
Enigma   31
First Embrace   32
Joy   33
Kindred   34
Linger   35
Love   36
Love is . . .   37
Magma   38
Mercy   39
Mirage   40
Nighthawk   41
Perfection   42
Resurrection   43
Rules   44
Summer   45
The Embrace   46
The Hum   47
Three Wishes   48
There You Were   49
Touched   50
Wanton   51
Where Was I Not to Notice You?   52

Lessons

Alternate Reality   55
Cat and Mouse   56
Chains of Pain   57
Controlling the Illusion   59
Cut Off   60
Darkness   61

Deceptive Angel   62
Death Worms   63
Deception Reflection   64
Deception or Truth   65
Fafnir   66
Fate   67
Forsaken Treasure   68
I Hate You   69
Lie   70
Lies   71
Lucifer's Deceit   72
Monster   73
Not Love   74
Plunder   75
Puzzle   76
Rockslide   77
Shattered Dreams   78
Sin   79
Superficial Love   81
The Beast   82
The End of My World   83
The Light   84
To Kill a Baby's Soul   85
Velvet Darkness   86
Why?   87

Gifts

Ajax   91
Babies Are Made Of . . .   92
Broken Baby   93
Christmas Every Day   94
Dynasty   96

Edelweiss   97
Frigg   98
Little Britches   99
Hau'puehuehu, This Is for You   100
He Mahele O' Kuu Puu Wai   101
He Mahele O' Kuu Puu Wai, This Is for You   102
Hercules   103
Hoa Aloha   104
Illyria   105
Kilinahe   106
Kittenish   107
Ko'i'ula   108
Lililehua   110
Lullaby   111
Ma'o Hau Hele   112
Odin   113
Pohakea   114
Polani   115
Polu   117
Ripley   118
Rubens' Beauty   119
Snowdrop   120
Sorsha   121
Squish and Squeak   122
Tiger Lily   123
Tiny Princess   124

Thoughts

Boredom   127
Life   128
Rules   129

Quotes by Masters   130
A Quote From My Daughter   131

Community

Bullies   141
Be Perfect   142
Cat's Paw   143
Cocooned   144
Darkness Incarnate   145
Defilement   146
Dipsomaniac   147
Embrace Your Gifts   148
False Gods   149
Freedom   150
Greed   152
Haunted   153
Heavy Hands   154
Match of the Siege   155
Mothers   156
Not Learning   157
Notion   158
Oligarchy   159
Punishment   160
Shades of Blue   161
Starlet   162
Stronghold   163
Self-Respect   164
Stop   165
Trust   167
Unreal World   168
Vote   169

Faith

Belief   173
Casting Stones   174
Hope   175
Insignificant   176
Inoa Po   177
On the Mountain   178
Perhaps   179
The Guff   180

Otherworldly

Awareness   183
Birth   184
Clarity   185
Compelled   186
Falling   187
God's Finger   188
Metal   189
Midnight   190
Nocturnal Anguish   191
Query   192
Shapeshifter   193
Vampir   194
Waking   195
Yod   196

Deities

Cyprus   199
Fire, War, and Love   200

Freya   201
Wisdom   202
Valkyrie   203
Vix Hellion   204

Nature

A Window into Their World   207
Aloha   208
Ballad of the Wanderers   210
Bloodlust   211
Buckaloose   212
Cloud Nursery   213
Forest Jewels   214
It's Going Off   215
K-23   217
Ki'i Pohaku   218
King of the Skies   219
Kure   220
Nene   221
The Kissing Ball   222
Overstepping Humans   223
Prairie Wolf   224
Papahanaumokuakea   225
Rebirth   227
The Aegean Sea   229
The Blue-Ringed Octopus   230
Wisdom We Can Learn from Wolves   231
Wheel of Life   232
Wolf Star   233

Dream

Curtain Wall   237
Panthera   238
The Vision   239

Multihued Rainbow

Blacksmith and Steel   243
Datsun 510   244
Enveloped in Darkness   245
Iron Rose Posse   246
Milo   248
Ovidia   249
Wild Card   252
Vixen   254

Stories

The Caterpillar   259
The Star   260

References   263
Glossary   265
About the Author   269

Looking Glass

Aniani

Awakening

Internal ecstasy

Longing washes over me

Bathing in it

Intoxicating

Reverent reluctance

Awaken

Bleeding

Glad tidings taken by a rakehell

Bitter endings cast a shadow of darkness, weaving
regret into the journey

An inky sadness permeates memories, clouding
perception and joy

Despair weighs heavily on the soul like storm clouds
blotting out the sun

Dimming the stars twinkling in the night heavens

Bleeding for a new beginning

Bloodsong

A fluttering of an essence dancing on the wind

Metallic lilies

Blood song, blood sings

Driven lost found

Complete

Caged

Wild at heart

Yearning to run free

Caged heart

Restraint released

Run free

Run wild

Half-Breed

Neither dark nor light

Shrouded in the fall

Forgotten existence

Solitary

Bringer of balance

Ekolu

Fragrant aromas waft on the many currents of *makani*. *Pikake*, ethereal and pure. Pakalana, strong, charismatic. Puakenikeni's evolving hues, ever changing and captivating. Three single strands of flowers interwoven into a garland of *pua*. Intoxicating scents fill the senses. Singular, beautiful, blended, overwhelming. *Pikake* and pakalana complement each other with melding fragrances. Puakenikeni independently is an extraordinary bouquet.

Hand Glass

A glimpse of my reflection saddens me

The repulsive reflection, an upwelling of tears

Breathe

Years of ridicule bounce off the dressing glass

Echoes of hate permeate

Breathe

The yoke of disgust and self-loathing is heavy to bear

Society's judgement looms over me

Breathe

If only I could love myself

Tears splash off the hand glass

Ho'oponopono

Foolery forgotten and forgiven

Harmony restored through reconciliation

Healing through love and gratitude

Open hearts met with tremendous gratitude

Iron Sanctuary

Taste of salt

Sound of metal grating

Old-school pain

Feeling of perspiration beading

Inner peace reclaimed

Leo

Birthed on the cusp

Shrouded in Cancer's shell

Birth of Leo is unrecognized

Marked by Regis

Misjudged cub

Little Faith

Little faith for one who fell

Gifted with sight but blind

Swathed in the Cimmerian shade

Murkiness illuminated

Eclipsed by an angelic embrace

Lost

Lost soul

Gifts stripped away, who are you now

Do you accept love and support or turn inward

Blossom or burn

Memory

Bronze angel

Subtle acceptance

Tender envelopment

Drink deeply

Belonging

True blood ties

Daughter

Feral Child

Intrinsic behavior forgotten

Anguish supplants exuberance

Persistently misunderstood

Attracts hellish devils

Desperately seeking to be loved

Roar of the Surf

Sunrise invokes cheer, warming the senses

Wakefulness comes slowly, like lapping waves
awakening hollowness

Illusive fulfillment of self lost in the foam and froth

Pulled out to sea, floating with the current unknowing
aspiration

Only the pounding of breaking surf is discernible

Salty tears of sadness ebb

Rousing

The descent forgotten

Longing lost

Wandering

Awareness haunting corners of the mind

No memories of the descent

No understanding of longing

No sense of self

Beacon

Intoxication

Connection made

Revelation true

The Angels Cried

I am in a sea of sorrow

The waves crashing over my head

The heavens sundered with the angels' cries as my soul
tore

The angels screamed in sorrow and for mortal
selfishness

Twilight

Enchanting amber horizon

Facades fade

Bleeding of chaos

Rebalancing of self

Love

Aloha

Allure

Drawn to his inner light

Compelling as a fiery storm

Powerfully wrought

Alluring

Bliss

A flicker of raw power

A quiet hallway

Sinewy grace emerges

Rippling under a sun-kissed surface

Caressed by a cloud

Focus falters

Concentration shattered by admiration

Painful bliss

Breathtaking

Looks so rare and regal

Flawless features, mesmerizing to gaze upon

Auburn hair, untamed and free

Olive skin radiating inner strength

Wisdom reflected in his speech

The gait of an athlete

Jaw-dropping gorgeous

Breathtaking

Broken Solitude

Progression breaks the solitude

Adrenaline courses through the stratum of bliss

Engulfing all reason

Buckling to the rapture in cardinal prayer

Burning

Gasp for air

Spellbound

Stop and stare

Smoking hot

Butterfly Kisses

Soft and gentle teasing

Pillow lips part with desire

Promise of velvet kisses

Double-Edged Blade

Lethal but enticing

Benevolent but merciless

Tender but ferocious

Ruthless with a moral code

Unfathomable creature of extreme intelligence

Dreams

His face haunts my dreams

Known but not known

Blazing smiles

Sculpted perfection

Radiating power and virility

Heart-stopping brilliance

Dream . . .

Enigma

Blindsided by exhilaration

Fierce warrior

Admiration and trust blossoms

Dangerous and alluring

An enigma

First Embrace

Consumed by searing need

Lavishly devouring pillowed flesh

Languishing in the taste of sweetness

Pleading whispers

A slow insatiable embrace

Joy

Laughter permeates the soft breeze

Longing intensifies with the brilliance of the sun

Joy

Kindred

Consuming all thought

Moments and waiting

Pulses dance with a relentless surging

Excruciating yearning

Merciful refuge sought

Intertwined completeness

Tempered storm

Linger

An unexpected kiss on the cheek

My breath caught, I couldn't breathe

The feeling still lingers on my cheek

Hope . . .

Love

Breathtaking

Perfection

Burning

Love is . . .

Love is . . .

Dumb by enchantment

Deaf by the heart roar

Blind by the fairy glamour

Mute by the pixie dust

Magma

Rising heat from the caldera floor

A metallic wind

The imparting of wisdom

Random acts of kindness

Molten rock sculpted into perfection

Insatiable desire

Unclaimed prize

Mercy

Combustible coincident

Blinding brilliance

God have mercy on my soul, to gaze upon such grace

Grant me compassion

Mirage

Heat waves shimmer through the atmosphere

Embers dance, igniting flesh

Enchanted by the flames

Engulfed

Rescue me

Nighthawk

Hidden

Caught in the snare

The touch of magic

Shining glory

Ride the wind

Perfection

In the chaos of the daytime, I stood still

Captivated by his presence as he glided across my path

Sent by angels

Brilliant as the summer sun

Resurrection

Gentle charm

Soft coaxing

Unexpected resurrection

Intoxicating anguish

Enveloped in awakening

Rebirth

Rules

Rules broken, castaway

Anticipation ignited

Go slowly, patiently, enticing

Breathe life into me, bring me to my knees

Glorious collision

Step across the line

Woo me

Beg me

Claim me

Summer

Mesmeric presence

Primal instinct

Insatiable longing ignited

Pull me closer

Summer brush my lips

Entangled

The Embrace

Rodin sculpted you

Chiseled your immaculate frame and features in perfect symmetry

Awestruck in your masculine grace

God gifted you to Beauty to connect on the eternal plane

Love that is so compelling and complete

In return you embraced Beauty, enveloping her

Treasured for all time, given completely to each other

Two sculptures intertwined forever in Rodin's stone

The Hum

The hum of feathers

A stealthy confidence

The rush of wind

A captivating presence

Moonlit radiance

Silent protector

Three Wishes

Ethereal music in a sterile world

An archangel's blinding brilliance

Caressing your soul

Defiance blooms among the filth

Intoxicating gaze

Heaven sent

Among routine

Achilles reincarnate

Driven, visionary, insightful

There You Were

There you were among the law books and benches

There you were in the night shadows

There you were astride thunder

There you were in the rain and haze

There you were unexpectedly in the maze

There you were flowing chaos

There you were among the fireworks and fumes

There you were a hypnotic vision in the rain

There you were gliding on the currents

There you were striking and stunning

Here you are

Touched

You touched my soul

You taught me how to play

You kissed my toes

My god of love

Wanton

Wanton touch

Passion ignited

Unrestrained desire

Demolished mirage

Shangri-la lost

Where Was I Not to Notice You?

The clouds lifted and there he was

Stunning in appearance

Brilliance radiating through him

Flaws made flawless in his splendor

My eyes drink in the sight of him, never tiring of gazing
upon him

Gorgeous

Lessons

Ha'awina

Alternate Reality

Entangled alternate reality

Memory exploited to punish

Painted as self-serving

Without validation

Quicksand of truth

Intentional snare

Rationalizing your actions to an audience

Is not reality

No one to champion

Constantly scrutinized

Dehumanized, challenged

How to make oneself whole

Lash out or walk away

Cat and Mouse

While the mouse was at home, the cat played

You wanted your cake and wanted to eat it too

You know the consequences of your actions

Why cry over spilled milk

Chains of Pain

Chains of pain

A child's dreams imprisoned

Shackled by blood

Chains of pain

Caged pursuits of purpose

Perverse pleasure in denial

Chains of pain

Sabotaged accomplishments

Gleeful celebration of pursued failure

Chains of pain

Price for misjudgment

Lineage is inescapable

Chains of pain

Eternal punishment

Never relinquishing the reins

Chains of pain

Will-o'-the -wisps

Kin and clan

Controlling the Illusion

Make her pretend

Give her the illusion of closeness

Dismantle her, diminish her, frighten her

Put upon to listen to her, punish her, ignore her

Rule her by a dictatorship

Consume her

She deserves my wrath

He is seduced by his anger

He is the master of confabulations

No, warmth, no flexibility, no interest in her, no belief
in her, no shared tasks

The spell reigns supreme

A pornographic stare

Seduction in secret

A shattered spell

Arsenic angel

Go to hell

Cut Off

Love lies bleeding

Rivelts pulse forth

Aching, pushed to pain

Warm puddles of life

Drowned in a metallic haze

Comfort and peace found

Darkness

Probing relentlessly, loathsome appendages

Hiding in the shadows

To what purpose?

Murky depths of self-deception

Dawn rises and retches from such a vile sight

Slink back, find comfort in your dark realm

Let go, know your role

Leave the dawn

Deceptive Angel

Master of deceit

Seductive and cruel

Binds love

Cunning and persuasive

Traps love

Conceited self-worship

Abuses love's heart

Loathsome and vile

Essence crusher

Despicable and traitorous

Repulsed love fades

Love lost

Death Worms

Hidden beneath the shifting sands

Meddlesome serpents

Spitting a corrosive stream of venom at their prey

The day is theirs, deceptive talebearers

Spike like projections entangled, unable to distinguish a beginning and end

The atmosphere crackles with electricity searing their mark

A devouring dance of tails fighting for purchase

Painstakingly constricting every gasp for redemption by their victim

Crimson stains sully the surface of the desert floor

Intertwined fates consume

Victory is elusive

Deception Reflection

Deceiver, you're deceiving yourself

Your memory is convenient when it serves your actions

Changing the past to soothe your own guilt

Accept responsibility for your own actions

Move on and learn from your mistakes

Growth and understanding will then come to bear
witness

Deception or Truth

The truth is shrouded in the mists

The mists lay between us

The truth is shadowed in the low-lying clouds

Until the brilliant warm sun burns away the swirling
mists, the truth will never be known

The mists will forever shroud the truth

Fafnir

Hoarding your possessions

Possessed by glittering coins

Losing the one thing you cannot buy

. . . love

Fate

Mankind strives for its own Armageddon

Until mankind strives for peace there will be no heaven
on earth

Forsaken Treasure

Forsaken treasure thrown away for a moment or
moments

Cruel, bitter, vile thing

Uncaring and selfish

Bile rises, choking the burning embers of passion and
love

Venom extinguishes heart's blood

Poison drips into the veins and life ceases to exist

Did you ever care or was it all a lie

I Hate You

I don't care

You're a nag

You ask too much

I don't want to do anything

I don't want to be near you

I hate you

Your love is twisted

Lie

Cloaked in kindness

Intentionally misguided

Accusatory self-righteousness

Deceptive solutions

Dark wisdom

Selective memory

Superior self-worth

Unfettered friendship

Paths parted

Lies

Look into my eyes

No soul

No humanity

Only lust and greed

Lucifer's Deceit

Demonic angel clothed in angelic beauty

Misleading prophecy

Seeking love, found darkness and despair

Revelation not harm

Found happiness and light

Monster

Acts of outrage, justified by impaired knowledge

Gain from misfortune, shameless self-imposed reason

Insensitive, boastful, and rash

Clever and calculating to his own means

Stingy despot, acts of selfishness justified

Self-indulgent appetite for touch, praised for his
wickedness

Congenital brute living by his senses alone

Immature self-lover

A soul in peril

Not Love

Badgering, not listening

When will you stop

Broken record, underhanded probes

When will you get it

Obsessive, controlling, rewriting history

Stop, move on

Go in peace

Plunder

Innocence absconded inescapably violated

Lured by friendship defiled by selfishness

Refusing to be denied, muffling pleas

Pillaged of joy, sickened by the act

Empty of passion

Puzzle

Callus assumptions

Careless criticism

Condescending recklessness with words

Deep-seated roots

Image tattered and torn to pieces

Unable to piece the puzzle back together, broken,
shattered

The game placed in the box and shelved, given up

Dust gathers on the lid, forgotten

Remove the box from the shelf

Dust bunnies float like snowflakes

Kindness rebuffed

Gentleness brushed aside

Belief improbable

Glimmers of laughter, trust perhaps

No . . . impossible

Rockslide

Lured into the silky strands

The promise of peace in the black widow's web

Only to find the agony of death in her clutches

On the cliff's edge it begins crumbling underfoot

My world crumbles and the land gives way, falling into
the depths of despair

Falling in a rockslide

Tumbling amongst the sticks and stones that break my
bones

Her words can hurt me

Amongst the rubble, crimson rivulets flow and the pain
is replaced with a sense of peace

Shattered Dreams

I am drowning in sorrow

It's hard to breathe

The air is thick with regret and pain

I can't fill my lungs with the air necessary to sustain life

Drowning in tears

Choking desperation

Waves crashing over my head

Drifting down, down, down to the bottom

Warm comforting soft sand welcomes me invitingly
into her grasp

As the cold pain washes over me, sea foam washes
ashore

Sin

War rages in the heavens

Lust overpowers love

The cold and calculating serpent banishes the light

Deceitful angel cloaked in illusion

Silky smooth words of hollow promises hook
unconditional love

The soft violet light caresses the sky with its velvet
touch

The heavens sparkle with love

Dark ominous clouds slowly creep over and swallow
the light

Insatiable greed, unholy use of the dead

Gluttonous in its cravings

It takes for granted unconditional love

The hunter slaughters the foundations of love

Pride's pawn is consumed in wrath

The sky shrieks in pain, the wind howls in anguish

Thunder reverberates, lightning sunders the heavens

The never-ending battle rages on

Deceptive and cunning sloth drains the light

Misuse of the light

Extinguishes the light

Creatures of the hell realm creep into the world

Angelic sword and shield protect the light

Love eludes you as you gaze into the mirror of self-worship

Driven relentlessly with the sole purpose of self-reign

Destroying the queen

Angel, demon

Do you regret your fall from grace

Only what you want matters

The downfall of man

Broken souls

Archangel, fallen angel

Superficial Love

Object for display only

Treated as less than human

No consideration

No compassion

No loving care

Loved by a superficial heart

Discarded for something more appealing

The Beast

Bloodlust drives it relentlessly

Blood drips from its fangs, splashing like tears on the earth

Not caring what flesh it rips apart in its rage

Only that its insatiable hunger is satisfied at all costs

Not caring what it kills, only of single-minded conquest

Driven relentlessly throughout time to satisfy its hunger

Primal bloodlust remains

The End of My World

She makes me sick

I make myself sick

I hate her

I hate myself

I want to be rid of her

I'll set her free

I'm free

I'm empty

Elation

Death

The Light

You tried to extinguish the flame

Now the light is gone

You are in the dark

To Kill a Baby's Soul

Don't love it in the womb, it can feel it

Wish it dead on its early arrival into the world

Even though it cries for its mother

Skinning its knees on the incubator walls

Someone loves it through its desperate struggle to
survive

As it grows, ridicule it

Crush its dreams

Destroy its trust

It clings to life

With all the pain it desperately wishes for someone to
love it and understand it

In its tortured soul anguish is constant

Why couldn't you love me, Mother

Wasn't I good enough for you

Why won't you love me

Why do you hate me

Velvet Darkness

The velvet darkness envelops the heart, consuming it

Sadness seeps in raven rivulets poisoning promises

Ruby-red tears of anguish stream into desolation and
pain

Hopes miserable death

Besotted fool

Why?

Why is it so hard for you to understand I don't need to
be with anyone

I am fine being alone

Why do you have to send me hate mail and say mean
things to me

Is it all a game

You broke the trust between us, that is irreparable

I forgive you

Please forgive me

I release you

Gifts

❦

Makana

Ajax

Hidden beneath rubble

Slowly fading from existence

Warrior's bite

Clan protection renounced

Nursed from the brink

Welcomed by Odin and his queen

Odin's tagalong

Kith and kin

Babies Are Made Of . . .

Waterlilies and rubies

Sugar and ice

Snowflakes and lion cubs

Broken Baby

Lioness wishes

Broken baby

Soft as an angel's wings

Cougar cuddles

Brave baby

Precious nuzzles

Little one sent from above

Snuggle baby

Christmas Every Day

Little *ohana* nestled between blue coats and angels

Sheltered by metal and the love that binds

Patriarch's roam their territory fraught with danger

Seeking a lofty vantage point in an atmosphere of
inaina

Evil lurks in the darkness, claiming nine lives

An abandoned gift from the most holy day of the year

Always a welcomed greeting, cheering the *puu'wai*

Waiting patiently, invoking Christmas exaltation

The court of the firstborn herald the illusive queen

Merry and bright halves usher in glad tidings

Magical savior and his little band of faithful

Neighborly *kokua* gratefully embraced

The '*uhane* of the holidays live year round

Dedicated to my little *kolone popoki*: Crooked Tail, Mr. Ears, Mommy, Cat Daddy, Keagan, Deidre, Achilles, Lincoln, Sadie, Quinn, Dagney, Baby Crooked Tail, and Devon

Nalowale: Skinny, Oreo, and numerous little ones

Ho'opakele 'ia: Ajax, Daisy, Rose, Bob, Calvin, Ziggy, Greer, Tigerlily plus two na keiki pipi

Special thanks to Lex and Karen.

Apono a cat in need of a forever home. Contact Kat Charities:
98-1268 Kaahumanu Street
202, Pearl City, HI, 96782
808-650-1234
info@katcharities.org

Dynasty

The queen taken before her time, leaving her king and whelps behind

Rock to his kingdom and devoted to his lost queen, newborns raised by a fatherly king

Kindred to the pack, dainty beauty swathes in silver and white, the last of her line

Gentle giant Thor, regal and dignified, inherits the dynasty

Avid huntress, Skaoi, the embodiment of winter, elegant and serene as a soft snowdrift

Sumarr escaped death, taken in by ancient pedigree, awaiting her turn to sit on the Emerald Throne

Bound together by succession

Edelweiss

Striking blue cornflower eyes from her native land

A sporting clip of apricot locks

In an infamous first meeting, the king was captivated
with her fun-loving banter

He climbed the treacherous rocky icy ledges and snowy
peaks to fetch the flower of emperors and kings gifted
to his Queen of Hearts

Chivalrous devotion reflected in a wreath of white
leaves interwoven with yellow and orange petals

Love personified

Frigg

Fate's arrival greeted by tears and anguish

Comforted by unabashed trust

Foreknowledge and wisdom of the wyrd

Odin's wife hailed from the wetland halls of Fansalir

Beloved one

Odin's kisses welcome to the Volker wanderer

United, treading their terrain

Clamoring up trees, preying upon avians, and basking
in the rays of the sun

Deep bonds of comradery sealed with affection

Unchangeable course of fate, unable to save Odin,
loving support

Departure of adored lord to Valhalla

Sassy seer weaving threads of fate

Wandering weaver blessing a new hearth

Peace and love

Little Britches

Dashing and darting to and fro

An inquisitive look and off she goes

Dainty and sure-footed sprite

Nuzzling and snuggling all night

Hau'puehuehu, This Is for You

This is for you, *hau'puehuehu*

Adorned with a reddish crown

Bejeweled in diamond dust

A gaze of stellar blue ice

Cloaked in pink and gold

Serene as snowfall

A unique prism of ice and frost

Sweet tempered with fierce inner strength

Hau'puehuehu I hold you dear

My rare little angel

He Mahele O Kuu Puu Wai

God's hand tore off a piece of my heart

It did not cause pain

It brought me everlasting joy

It brought me the gift of insight

It brought compassion and caring for one another

It brought sensitivity back into balance

And God stayed, bringing peace and love into the world

He Mahele O' Kuu Puu Wai, This Is for You

He Mahele O' Kuu Puu Wai, this is for you

Llio holo I ka uaua whispered of your arrival

Birthed in serenity and splendor

Crowned with a majestic chocolate mane

Tender-hearted lad

Emanating warmth like the sun's rays seeping into your heart

Gallant knight of sagacity

Herculean physique crafted by the gods

Gift of reflection

Faithful and bold

He Mahele O' Kuu Puu Wai, I hold you dear

My rare panther Leo

Hercules

Fate is a strange thing

Preconceived judgement has a way of haunting you

Your family left you behind without hesitation

Subjecting you to torment and trauma

Sulking in the shadows for scraps

I recognized you in the dim light

Cautiously staying on the outskirts, fending for yourself

Companionless gentle giant

Friendship found, only to be lost by false promises

A gaze sears my soul, haunting me

You won my heart

Hoa Aloha

Pulelehua, transformed in the ancient archipelago and
thrived

Drawn to taste the of the koa's sweet nectar

Your natural beauty camouflages you in the koa forest

Hina's fringe wing dancing in the treetops

Ponumomi, little *'ula'ula* and *ele'ele* luck charm

A blessing to those she encounters

Brightening the day, disrupting the darkness

Teaching belief in yourself and to dare to fly

Pu'eo, protector and guardian

A deep connection between heaven and earth

You see what others cannot

Bringer of luck and wisdom

A hui hou

Ilyria

Invaded by inhumane invaders, inflicting torment

Traversing her vast territory to protect her hidden brood

Her flight was as swift as a Liburnian galley skimming
on the Mediterranean Sea

Her newfound sanctuary, kindred coddled

Her origins forgotten, spectral scars of fear remain

War-torn beauty, soothed by her new prince

Protective shelter, Odin embraced

A plummeting tumble, rescued by the wisdom of Frigg

Her ethereal movement like rhinos in a deep forest,
haunting the edge of shadows

Keening loss of love, but love not lost

Ever so slowly unraveling her cocoon of vigilance,
succumbing to tenderness

Surveying her kingdom, nestled in her roost

Breathtaking elegance, omniscient emerald eyes

Captured hearts

Kilinahe

Hello little one, we haven't met yet

I can't wait for you to arrive when the veil is the thinnest

Blessed by Danu, fey blood courses through your veins

Your beauty is of legend

Your glossy locks will be tossed by the soft gentle winds

Your eyes will reflect like the gentle rain on the face of the lehua blossoms

The sweetness of your voice will resonate with the melodic sound of the beloved fine light rain

Your graceful movements will echo the pleasant patter of rain splashing on the laua'e ferns

I look forward to cradling you in my arms, tiny princess

My heart swells with love for you

Kittenish

Wistful elegance, when no one is watching she blossoms

Troublemaking Einstein always working an angle

Lighthearted and rambunctious Finn, ever ready to play

Pixieish itsy-bitsy has plenty of moxie

Peering out from the safety of cover, the fainthearted hulk

Spritely beauty with her ever-cautious way

Koʻula

I never imagined how much love would fill my heart
when I saw you

I was spellbound by your sky-blue hypnotic gaze

You transformed my soul

The bears foretold of your birth, forever protected by
ice and snow

Pretty baby, skin as soft as a swan's feathers

A luminous inner light that is spellbinding

An de shealladh flows within you

The vibrant pink thistle connotes your lineage and
fortitude

You are as beautiful as the rainbow-hued rain of Napili

Descended from the celestial ladder into my arms

Tears filled my eyes as my heart swelled with a
boundless love for you

Unique as a sunbow in the misty rain and radiant as a multihued opal

Me ke aloha pumehana

Lililehua

Aloha, Lililehua

Belonging to the uplands and plains

Caressed by the wind, your misty soft showers
replenish

Your tiny droplets rest on the rare hakea blossoms

Lightly showering my face with your love

Lullaby

Gifts from God
Touched by the heaven
Eyes like pieces of the sky
Hair kissed by the sun
Snowflakes and daisies
Eternal sunshine
Angel baby

Gift from God
Touched by heaven
Eternal sunshine
Angel babies

Gift from God
Touched by heaven
Tawny eyes of a lion cub
Wild ebony locks teased by the wind
Starfire and warm gentle rain
Eternal sunshine
Angel baby

Gift of God
Touched by heaven
Eternal sunshine
Angel babies

———

Ma'o Hau Hele

Caressed by the wind, the hardy and brilliant blossom dances

Bathed by the morning dew, droplets glisten off delicate petals

Endearing to become the perfect companion to Waikakalaua

Anchoring *aina* and *lani*

A laudable union of a brightly woven garland made of golden flowers and a burst of *pala'a*

Strong unbending flower tempered by the verdant aroma

Willfulness shown against the wind, Lililehua

Tempered by the rain, Leikoko'ula

Beautified through the eyes of motherhood

Meddled into *ohana*

Odin

Patient and tender

Yearning endearment

Exquisite soul

Hearth found

Joyous, triumphant

Snuggle of gratitude

Overwhelming sense of love

Savior

Little prince

Pohakea

Prayers answered from the across the Pacific Ocean

Presentiment from Asia of an impending arrival

An uncle's gift bestowed with heartfelt love

German shepherds wait patiently on the sandy beach as
the dawn breaks the horizon

Sunlight bursts forth, birthing the sun, greetings barked
by devoted companions

Rays of light glint off their glossy black and tan coats

Forever loyal protectors of the dawn

Polani

A vision of beauty from the netherworld

The tiny siren's graceful features are enchanting

Cradled in seafoam, rocked by the undulating waves

The merrow's bewitching siren is embraced

She is a force of nature from two realms

Her ancient roots, stemming from Melusine with two
tails and Neptune

Her melodic cries are broken with a whale bone rattle, as
shimmering pearl tears trickle down her flawless cheeks

Her chubby baby hands attempt to grasp at the tiny fish,
bringing forth her lyrical laughter

Melodic songs resonate from her lips, skittering off the
ocean's surface

Her alluring song will call forth storms and lure hearts

Her intelligence will challenge a man's skill

Her tail will propel her swiftly through the depths,
avoiding capture

For now, the Outer Hebrides palace shelters the tiny sea maiden

Nestled in ribbons of kelp, frolicking with the sea otters

Basking on the coral reef, as a soft breeze dances through the tendrils of her hair

Destiny awaits the little queen

Polu

Trapped in the gallows

Beckoning for release

Wrenched heartstrings

Companionship sought

Padlocked affection

Peekaboo acceptance

Fevered tenderness melts the heart

Enduring love

Ripley

Queen of her carpet kingdom

Bounding bursts of speed from dusk to dawn

Displays of agility and grace, stalking her prey across the carpeted savannah

Patrolling the grasslands, concealing herself in the rattan forest

Greetings expressed in a multitude of meows, head rubbings, and sandpaper kisses.

Bravery and prowess demonstrated with a repertoire of intense snarling and hissing

Reigning over her kingdom from atop the cardboard cliffs

Basking in the sun

Lounging at the steel watering hole

All is well in her kingdom

Rubens' Beauty

Rubenesque beauty painted by a master

Your grace forever captured on canvas

Women envy you, men agonize over you

Your flawless ivory skin, cinched waist, and voluptuous
curves

My lovely lounge lizard, did he find you on a couch in
Luxembourg

Did he lure you to the canvas with his superstar status
or entice you in other ways

With his masterful strokes he immortalized you in all
your glory

Rubenesque beauty, adorning walls for centuries

Rubens, we still applaud your genius

Snowdrop

Light as down

Drifting down from heaven, caressing the wind with
delicate grace

Gliding on the currents, tousled and teased by the wind

Pristine tiny etched ice sculptures

Each unique in all aspects

Angelic beauty

God's frozen tears, snowdrops from heaven

Snowdrops drifting down to Mother Earth to sooth her
sorrow and pain

Tender soft kisses of love from her child

Bathing her in God's love

Sorsha

Always a warm greeting

A nibbling kiss

A gentle nudge

A soft bark for love

A penetrating stare

Filled with love and knowing

A comforting head resting on your lap

Healing your soul

Thunderstorm cuddles

Fireworks shared by three

Gentle giant full of grace

Striding alongside a goddess

Regal stature born of centuries past

Lounging on historic beauty

My princess

The queen

My rock

Squish and Squeak

Squish and squeak

Ooze and melt

Ever watchful, wistful beholding

Delicate constitution, wary curiosity

Closet cavern, lofty perch

Rough and tumble

Pounce and prey

Frolicking cohorts

Devoted kin

Tiger Lily

Delicate whimsical creature that can traverse the bridge
between earth and sky

Herald of Apollo, transformed in Hyperborea

Moonlight illuminates her majestic beauty

Elegantly long-limbed

Her soul speaks of tranquility and gentleness

Fairness of Aphrodite with the power to charm gods
and queens

Last of her brood, she captured my heart

Tiny Princess

Merciless act committed

Cruelly tossed into oblivion

The fall's impact breaking her

Her littermate was not so lucky

Cuddled next to her cold sibling

Broken, crying for her mother

Terrified, she hides in damp darkness

Beckoning coos draw her to comfort

Bedraggled and injured

Toted with gentleness

Feisty fighter

Welcomed with love

Nuzzling, she finds solace

Thoughts

Mana'o

Boredom

Boredom is a state of mind, which you can control.
Boredom is a choice.

Life

When life knocks me down I get up, dust myself off, and trudge on.

Rules

You can't play with everyone in the sandbox, then get out and start throwing sand at everyone. Your playmates have every right to drag you back in the sandbox and bury you.

Quotes by Masters

Quotes by masters, disrespected or immortalized into song?

A Quote From My Daughter

Living the dream, sometimes it's a nightmare.

—Vraunwyn Denny

Contemplation

Noonoo ana

A father is larger than life to his *keiki*

A secret only remains a secret if it never passes through parted lips

A vehicle's horn is meant to announce imminent danger, not rage

Adversity bonds people who would not otherwise be

Ancient knowledge of frequencies and formulas for success used for greed, not shared for equality

Ashes to ashes
Dust to dust
Twenty-one ounces of stardust

Blue courage is going where everyone else is running from

Do not waste your time chasing love, let it come to you

Each one of us has the power to make a difference, to become the engine of change

Faith has been twisted through time by people in power to forward their own agenda

Fear creates monsters in the mind

Friends see the light before you do and still stay by
your side and wait until you do too

Greed is the downfall of mankind

Hate is the inability to put aside your differences to
work toward a common goal

Humans are the most destructive species on earth

I am one
Then I will be two
Then several

If you have good beat partners, you can work anywhere
in any conditions

It's a chick thing

It's not what you have but who you have around you
that matters

Law enforcement protects their own
They also devour their own

The ocean is a wilderness, enter it with respect and
caution

Leave this world a better place than it was when you
entered it

Music is a universal language that speaks to our DNA

People use being human as an excuse to have no morals
or values

Raise your children to see souls, not skin color

Ritual embracing of Armageddon is suicide for the
human race

Some people touch our heart and connect our souls

Succumbing to anger accomplishes nothing

The fallacious statement "thrown to the wolves" should
be "thrown to the savage humans"

The key to survival under stress is to not panic

Until we respect each other, there will always be hate

You can doubt climate change is real, but the proof is
evident when the world stopped because of COVID-19

Community

Kaiaulu

Bullies

Hurtful ridicule in adolescence leaves inner scars

Guttersnipes grown up, continuing to nip

Unchecked needler in adulthood

In the guise of supervision, harassment is encouraged and glorified

Blind eyes are turned in fear of drawing attention to themselves

Bullies shattering lives without consequence

Blue culture behavior is socially acceptable

Ridicule is endless

Suck it up, buttercup

Allies are turncoats as you are ostracized

The ever-present heckler embraced

Falos talebearer

Demeaning mockery from a powerful position

Be Perfect

Stay in the moment

Focus, concentrate

Strive for perfection

Cat's Paw

Big guns, dispensable pawns

Brass selling the illusion of hard work, dedication, and loyalty

Falsehoods, false pretenses, only the golden children matter

Misappropriation of plunder

Looting to achieve their own agenda

Bottomless pillaging

Expendable cat's paw

No one cares about you

You are a means to an end

Cocooned

Living in their bubbles

Narcissistic ego beings

Close-minded, refuse to seek the truth

Believe what is being sold by the media without
question

Wrapped in their cocoons, they don't even notice the
world is in crisis

Destroy and move on

No thought of consequences

Only one planet for us all to live on

People and countries need to put hate aside

Do what is right for the planet

Darkness Incarnate

A malady birthed in torment

Ankle biters' twisted enthrallment

Forsaken tenderness, masked fiend

Pubescent nightmares lure

Masks of spirits and sniggering

Glistening viscera is intoxicating

To capture Adonis is fleeting

Walking the straight and narrow

Scholastics and camouflage

Parchment draws the malevolence forth

Window dressing and grave digging

Heinous insistent compulsion

Detached enthrallment, gruesome acts

Dispatched to the Netherlands

Defilement

Naivety of youth precedes predicament

Pinned, struggling against intended force

Tears cascading down flesh, gasping for air against the
pressure inflicted

Release is followed by cold silence and shock

Nonacceptance is the only path

A false friendship

Struggle for freedom, pleas to stop ignored

Inflicted bruising hidden beneath blues

Unfathomable shame

Silence

Self-loathing

Dipsomaniac

Knowledge used as a weapon

Betrayal of own kind

Petty payback meant to maim

Denial of own conduct

Intent to deface

I forgive you

Embrace Your Gifts

You may not want the gifts God gave you

Embrace them, you don't have a choice

False Gods

We worship the god box, with all its false *Gods*

We strive to emulate the false gods with their broken
vows, shattered morals and values

Mislead down the unfruitful path

We have lost our way

Freedom

So much hate directed at one person

Why

Misguided, uniformed

No rational thought

No pursuit of knowledge

You have the right to choose

You choose not to choose

Then blame without reason or knowledge

Make a choice

Support the choice that is made

Our commander in chief deserves our respect and
support

Have your own knowledgeable opinion

Vet your opinion with credible information

Acknowledge your freedom

Respect your freedom

Not everyone has the freedom to choose

It is a gift, use it well

Stop complaining and do

Greed

Racism born anew

Bred by greed

The soul forgotten, only skin color remains

Lack of determination breeds selfishness

Lines are dissolving

Clouds over

Darkening with sadness

Fueled by hate

Weep for our children

Is it worth it

The loss of humanity

Haunted

Was the risk worth it

Unrecoverable lost time

Upwelling of anguish

Numb and disconnected

Resilience and enduringness

Haunted

Heavy Hands

The atmosphere snaps

Fury sparks

Anger cracks

Erratic and fierce

Enraged beyond reason

Lashing out without remorse

Unspoken scars remain

Match of the Siege

Roman legacy

Birthed under siege

Battle instead of war

Birthright of red, white, green, and blue

Adorned in doublets and knickerbockers

Lions fighting side by side

Intertwined by tradition and honor

Defying the passage of time

Let the game commence

Fifty-minute brutal fray

Cheers and applause

Victory and prestige

A beautiful game

Mothers

Sometimes our mothers aren't there in the way we need
them to be

May not like us

May not live up to their expectations

May disappoint them

But never doubt they love us

We may love ourselves

We may live for our dreams

We may be proud of ourselves

Not Learning

We are still barbarians at heart, bent on the annihilation
of each other

No focus on the preservation of democracy, philosophy,
art, and culture

No learning from history, making the same mistakes

Notion

Why is it a preconceived notion that we automatically mature and have been taught the skills we need when we graduate from high school or college? Most things we weren't taught, and we are the same person. It's just a different day.

Oligarchy

Do they remember they serve the people

Hidden language of deceit drafted to serve themselves

Serving their own agendas

Punishment

Rush to package blame

Refracting truth in need of a scapegoat

Routine treatment rooted in fear

Mocking and humiliating

Resulting in tormenting shame

Shades of Blue

Survival's choice leads to sacrifice and resilience

The glittering warmth of the surface a brilliant shade of aquamarine

Lurking underneath silty depths blue cloudy waters

Heroes cloaked in authoritative navy

Villains cloaked by the shadowy deception of indigo

Oaths upheld by blue steel

Starlet

If your mom isn't there for you

You're not alone

Grow up

Be responsible

The world wants to see you stand up and succeed

Take control of your life

If you want your children

Stop disrespecting yourself

Believe in yourself

Hold your head high

It doesn't matter what people think

We believe in you

You are capable of great things

Stronghold

Injustice prevails within castle walls

Crumbling foundations are concealed by the finest
tapestries

The liege lord rules to a baneful court

Untrue natures crush the good Samaritan

Demise of the fortification forewarned

Nobles' contempt decried by the king of arms

Compassion and mercy abandoned

Devotion and loyalty dismissed

Finest favors bestowed tattered and torn

Friendships and allegiances forsaken

Harken broken bulwark

The dulled blue fortress cracks

Once shining, now lackluster

Fading kingdom

Self-Respect

The world doesn't owe you anything

Make something of yourself

Don't ride on you ancestors' coattails

Honor them

Honor yourself

Stop

Leave her alone

Give her space to heal and grow

Stand up and take control of your life

I know you can do it

It's painful to watch you crumble

If you want to be with your children

Fight for them

Children are resilient and forgiving

It's time to grow up

Be responsible

I know how it feels to be alone

Stop trusting in others

Trust yourself

Be cautious of people wanting to befriend you

They have ulterior motives

Greed

Stop disrespecting yourself

Be a lady

Be a role model

All of us have fallen down, dust yourself off and move
on

Live

Trust

Trust is elusive because you never really know
someone, because you will never know what someone
else is truly thinking.

Unreal World

Society disconnected from the real world

Distracted by the momentary fad

Insecure, falls prey to the deception of censorship

Follows blindly

Latches onto false promises without rational thought or knowledge

Results in disappointment and unfulfillment

Blame cycle

Stop, look inside

Seek out the real world

Vote

One voice

Can anyone hear it

Vote

Faith

Mana'o'i'o

Belief

Is it possible to believe in God without labeling oneself

Labeling is segregation, racism, and martyrdom

Why isn't belief enough

Casting Stones

Sinners cast stones without thought

Their glass houses forgotten

Blame cast cruelly, rippling like a stone skipping across
a pond

Sin's mirror reflection ignored

Harsh criticism cast for self-indulgence

Cast another stone

Hell's gates await

Sea of sorrow

Hope

Unexpected sunrise

The gentle morning sun breaths warmth into your soul

Hope . . .

Insignificant

Have you ever gazed at something so awe-inspiring and felt so insignificant?

Inoa Po

Swirling blue hues

Little soul waiting in the ethereal world

Ancestors' voices permeate the veil

Heed the night name

Given with aloha

On the Mountain

On the mountaintop I can feel God's warmth touch my face, as the comforting mists

Swirl around me in a loving embrace

Perhaps

Perhaps we are all angels

God waiting for us to choose the darkness or the light

Given the chance to choose, thus the demons are created

The Guff

The sparrows wait patiently to sing again

Promises from the guff

Love and hope to swell in their breasts with song

Otherworldly

Pualenaaaa

Awareness

Awareness breathes

The veil flutters

Haunting disbelief

Overwhelming comprehension

Longing evolves

Insatiable feeding

Euphoria

Revelation

Birth

Fallen and forgotten

Lost in darkness

Feel the hunger

Awaken

Clarity

The sliver of time just before dawn

When the darkness begins its slumber

When the light awakens

Clarity exists

Compelled

Looking so fine

Restraint and control

Longing for you

Sinner and saint

Pure of heart

Held first by honor and virtue

The grace waits

Endure the fall

Bestow heaven's angelic cry

Falling

Do you remember falling

Dust off

Unfurl your wings

Remember the light

Remember your chosen path

Fly

God's Finger

God's finger marks a preordained path charted in the
heavens

The battle rages against the relentless pull

Unfathomable mutual weakness reigns

Inevitably ethereal music is to be played

Unstoppable destiny

Metal

A penetrating stare consumed with undeniable hunger

Burning surrender melting in metal

Entangled mutual need

Agonizing pleas

Enticing flesh speaks of what's to come

Metal music

Midnight

Unwavering stare

Knowing, waiting

Scales black as midnight

Watching

Nocturnal Anguish

Shrouded in shadow

Shapeshifter reborn in Cimmerian shade

Night falls, eerie roost

Malevolence kindled with bloodlust

Undead creature, unnatural flight

Draconian love spell

Innocent babe in the woods, sacrificed prey

Harrowing transition heralds vampiric hunger

Enveloped in Tellus's lair

Query

The pendulum swings

The fallen's inquest echoes

Faith and trust in smithereens

Trust the celestial heavens

Release it

Be present in the juncture

Shapeshifter

A falcon's perch cloaked and adrift in the soft clouds

Protector and deliverer of souls

Bringer of dew and sunfire

Adorned in fruits of Vanir

Aloft the golden boar, enthralled by rapture

Tears of anguish wept in red gold and amber sprinkled
over the land

Fire of the enlightened one

Vampir

Awareness breathes

The veil flutters

Haunting disbeliefs

Overwhelming comprehension

Longing evolves

Insatiable feeding

Euphoria

Revelation

Waking

The descent forgotten

Longing lost

Wandering

Awareness haunting corners of the mind

No memories of the descent

No understanding of longing

No sense of self

Beacon

Intoxication

Connection made

Revelation true

Yod

A battles rages against the unstoppable force of God's finger's preordained path charted in the constellations.

Aspects of an unfathomable mutual weakness.

Inevitably, ethereal music is to be played.

Destiny

Deities

Akua

Cyprus

The sea moans as she wades the sandy shores

Fondled and embraced by the lapping tides

Caressed by the sea foam

Girdled by Olympus

Violet crowned beauty

Hypnotic

Fire, War, and Love

She walks in fire

Beauty and wisdom

Astride her chariot drawn by savage beauty

Steely grace

Freya

Strong-willed queen

Beautiful and fierce

Armor glittering in the morning sky

Grandeur waits above the battlefield

Clashing steel

Pick of the fallen

A flurry of wings

Hall of heroes

Wisdom

Athena's white owl, eloquent

Wisdom's knowing gaze

Zeus's merry eyebrows and gentle eyes reconfirming
life

Odin's penetrating gaze

His raven eyes pool liquid night

Sleek and glossy, takes flight

Valkyrie

Awakened relic

Astride thundering fury

Awaits the battle to come

Angelic warrior

Vix Hellion

Servant of Odin and Freya, the lily-throated Lady Vix Hellion, lover of heroes and winged guide to the slain. Flying over the battlefield, choosing who lives or enters the hall of heroes. Mounted on her steed, she is "ready to ride."

Nature

Kulohelohe

A Window into Their World

Elevated on earthen floors, ancient pedigree lounge

Nestled in tight balls on sparkling snowfields

Youngsters rouse, rested, ready for an enthusiastic
rollick

Ravens flutter just out of reach

A bison carcass awaits, for all members to satiate their
hunger

One by one the pack feeds, one by one they depart

Cresting the hill and off in an organized formation

Their kill nurtures coyotes, foxes, and eagles

Masterpieces crafted to perfection

Aloha

Precious lei of islands, you are in my heart

My beloved ancestral home brings a welling of tears

The fairest star cherished evermore

Your Koolau's soaring cliffs draped with rainbow-hued waterfalls

The scent of *lipoa* wafting on the sea breeze at Kawela Bay

Buff shores caress the sleeping *honu*

I yearn to bury my toes in your warm sands

Feel the sun kiss my skin

Inhale the fragrant blossoms tantalizingly drifting on the wind

Longing for your lush beauty, rich in *aina* and *moana*

Entranced by the *puahiohio* showers

Beguiled by the *pu'eo* floating on the currents of uplifting air

---

Adorned by the tiny *'a'ama* crabs skittering across the lava rocks

'Ilio-holo-i-ka-uaua frolicking in your sparkling aquamarine depths

Your unsurpassed beauty beckons to me

Precious lei of islands, you are in my heart

My beloved ancestral home brings a welling of tears

The fairest stars, cherished evermore

Ballad of the Wanderers

A ballad from antiquity reverberates

Harmonious notes

A symphony of earth

A cadence of destruction and creation

Comic balance, elegant spirals

Aria of innumerable worlds float in the universe

Overture of incineration

Perpetual winter, little by little

An ominous tempo beats

Waltz of no escape

Bloodlust

Consumed with terror

Running from the inevitable

Nowhere to hide

Defenseless to the aerial pursuit

Heart pounding with exertion

Muzzle slathered in froth

Ragged breaths rasping in her chest

Deafening shots ring out

Unfair advantage

Where's the hunt

No sport

No challenge

Brutal senseless killing

Man's cruelty

Pure slaughter

Bloodlust

Buckaloose

Living apart from the natural world

Out of harmony

Predators eliminated

Disease controlled

Resources plundered

Buckaloose

Stop consuming the earth

We are interwoven

Consuming with consciousness

Cease creating extinction

Make amends

Rewild nature

Be *akamai*

Cloud Nursery

The tippy-tops of the forest canopy cradle the newly formed clouds

In the valley of Waikakalaua ʻohu, the low-lying fog shelters the newborns

The sunlight dusts the *keikis* with rainbows

The wind, *makani* lulls the babies to slumber

Forest Jewels

Chattering of the akeke'e echoes *mauka* to *makai*

Under the forest canopy the *'i'iwi* nip at the lehua blossoms

As vaporous mist, Awa'awa smoothers the lehua blossom on the mountain cliffs

A little kiwikiu tilts its head, revealing its distinctive black eye strip as it whistles, signaling *lilani*, the unexpected rain

The beating of wings and rush of wind as the 'alalā take flight

A sudden shower bursts from the sky, pelting the 'ōhi'a leaves with a cold stinging rain

The *naulu* rain brings bitterness and sorrow to the native forest

Dampened flowers infused with rain are beaten down

Fluttering of feathers shake off raindrops sparkling in the morning sun

A cascade of shed dewdrops spray the ama'u ferns

A rainbow blooms across the caldera

It's Going Off

Dawn patrol ushers in biological annihilation

The Holocene epoch drops in

Species caught inside drown

Gremmies become big guns

Waiting in the lineup, there is a lull

Men in gray suits watch evolution unfold

Outside a set approaches rolling in, disrupting
adaptation and nature's balance

Peeling, spray is cast upward in sorrow

Charging, mankind's folly

Hit the lip, wake up

Goofy-footed, riding the steep face of annihilation

Making the bottom turn matters

Enlightenment in the barrel

Kicking out, desecration of biodiversity

Riptide of species loss

A grinder builds, a cascade effect felt

Its steep wall, the deck smacking the surface

The nose is beginning to pearl dive

Walk it back, self-balancing exists

Don't bail, hang loose

Eddie would go

Shaka brah

K-23

Nuzzled into the pillow-soft sand

Cradled by its warmth as she lounges on the shoreline

Warm steady breath

Sun-dried fur sprinkled with salt crystals begin to dampen as the gentle incoming tide laps at her hind flippers

Whiskers bristle at the salt spray

Hope

Ki'i Pohaku

Crowning brooding cliffs, peach stone sentinels

Beautiful ancient oddity

Unyielding, uncompromising

Staunch pillars of the stars

Cold, affectionless

Weathered menhirs

Revered

King of the Skies

Perched aloft the craggy tower of the stars

A glint of gold

Keen striking pale eyes

Ancient messenger silently foretells

Haunting shrieks

Soaring to the heavens a thunderous beating of plumage

Rapid descent of lightning to the unknowingly

Majestic splendor honored in bonnets and on cave walls

Only bested by the wren

Kure

On a downy soft beach

Rests the seal with its velvety sun warmed fur

Lounging on the shoreline

Warm steady breaths

Whiskers bristle in the salt spray

Nene

Gracing the summit of Mauna Loa

Arid and desolate lava fields shelter and protect

Bejeweled with a black crown and cream-colored
cheeks

Charismatic beauty of earth and sky

Ambling waddling on partially webbed feet

Soft greetings emitted, grumbles and hoots

Devoted nene

Nesting underneath the kipuka

Goslings camouflaged in the tall grass

White-rumped wily goose

Grazes the ʻōhelo berries

Ancient guardian

The Kissing Ball

Yuletide greenery blooms in winter's starkness

Frigg's tears transformed into pearlescent berries on its boughs, hailing peace and love

Refuge in all seasons for the likes of hawks and butterflies

Forest savior bringing hope to all

Allheal gathered with holy golden sickles, illuminated by a new moon sprig's fall from sacred oaks fluttering like snowflakes as they drift towards the snow-laden ground

Reverently caught in mid-flight by ancient cloaks from allheal-laden trees

A magical sight above bringing luck to revelers below

Timeless tradition ringing throughout the ages of friendship and goodwill

Heralding in rebirth, truces, and life everlasting

Little mistletoe evermore linked to Christmastime

Overstepping Humans

Where is the concern for the destruction of our home

Where is the urgency to halt the destabilization of earth

Wake up, the planet is dying

Prairie Wolf

The little western song dog

Candid mirror of humanity

Migrated the world with mankind

Remarkably adaptable prairie wolf

Admiration for the misunderstood trickster

Respect for coyote

May we learn from you

Papahanaumokuakea

Fiery path extinguished long ago
Forgotten kingdom, reminiscent of old
A treasure chest found nowhere else in the world

Jutting out of shallow waters, Moku Manu's vertical
cliffs and deep valleys are decorated with *loulu* and
'ohai. Hidden from sight in a rocky outcropping, a faint
wash of greenish-yellow plumage glimpsed, cherished
little songbird.

Mokumanamana, basalt hills dotted with ancient *ki'i*.
A fishhook rests, the dark glistening path of Ke Alanui
Polohiwa a Kane.

The crescent reef of Kanemiloha'i, vestiges of long-
cooled fires rest in the sea. On narrow shallow sandspits
and shoals bask *ilio-holo-i-ka-uaua*.

Beneath Puhahonu's peaks, behold underwater
pinnacles where 'opihi cling. Its rocky shores are
covered by a garland of akulikuli.

The linear coral gardens of Nalukalala radiate out
like rays of the sun. Sweeping waves pour into sandy
lagoons, clouding steep reefs with slit and sand.

Upraised old coral reefs of Kauo shelter intertidal pools. Beautiful white sand beaches crested with coastal grasses surround an interior lake filled with the buoyant bottom-up koloa. Translucent blue waters of a protected bay cradle birthing mano.

Papa'apoho torn asunder in the dawn of time. It's a coral bank vestige connected by a depression awash in a blue-green expanse. Gone are the guano and feather hunters. Vast shallow waters harbor an oasis for sea life.

Manawai and Holoikauaua are low-lying beauties only detectable as waves collide into a fringed reef in explosions of whitewash. Offshore, striking spinner dolphins burst forth from the ocean in aerial spirals.

Kawelu embellishes Pihemanu's landscape, trampled on by moli's ritual courtship dance of graceful dips and bows. Masters of the air currents, shrieks and shrills float down from speckled skies.

Mokupapapa, the crowning glory of the archipelago. Draped with *kauana'oa pehu* like a feather cape. Turquoise waters lap at pristine white sand beaches littered with seal pups. The last outpost in the realm of Po.

Rebirth

Sweet grasses and wildflowers beaten by the wings of
love warmed by the sun

Chosen words plant the seeds of doubt

Decay creeps slowly into the meadow of love, fouling
the earth with its taint

Innocently the wildflowers sway gently in the breeze
while the lynx and hare continue their eternal dance,
their fates intertwined

Eagles and hawks soar gracefully in the sky, nesting in
the trees surrounding the peaceful meadow so full of
life

Dark tendrils slither unknowingly through the warm
earth and slowly choke the life above

Decay and rot overpower the meadow, the lynx and
hare seek sanctuary elsewhere

Eagles and hawks leave their empty nests as the
meadow withers

Forgotten, full of silence

A storm brews in the heavens, thunder growls, and
lightning flashes in the sky

Lightning strikes, scorching and scaring the earth

The meadow's heart shrieks.

Sparks smolder, tendrils of flame ripple forth, igniting the deadfall

Rivers of fire roar forward and the meadow is engulfed in the blaze

Flames burn away the taint, leaving the meadow bare and exposed, ceasing to exist

A warm gentle rain begins to fall, nourishing the earth and extinguishing the blaze

The fire planted new seeds of life in its fury

Rebirthing the meadow

Tiny blades of new life begin to emerge from Mother Earth to start anew

The Aegean Sea

The Aegean Sea sparkling like liquid sapphires

The warm sun penetrates her depths refracting like jeweled facets

Dolphins break her surface in a radiant cascade of wet diamonds

Poseidon reigns her depths, roaming the realm on his gilded chariot

Guarding her shores, riding the sea foam's salty mist

The Blue-Ringed Octopus

Diminutive leviathan creeping and compressing to the rocky crags

Lithe and leggy huntress frolicking in the deep

Snared in the buccaneer's dragnet

Lethal neon blue rings glimmer through an inky sea

Swashbucklers take heed of your menacing inmate

Cleaver cephalopod, jet-propelled jailbreak a league under the sea.

Wisdom We Can Learn from Wolves

Adapt to your environment

Communication

Empathy

Loyalty

Play

Respect others

Rest

Take only what you need

Teamwork/cohesiveness

Trust your instincts

Valor

Wheel of Life

The Oak King concedes the darkest days to the Holly
King

The harsh winter's landscape decorated with shiny
green leaves and crimson berries

Refracting colors of light in the darkness

Eight stags await the promise of light

Reborn, the Oak King bids farewell to umbra

Yule gives way to life, and the green man

Twins reign in an everlasting battle of transformation

Brightest blessing in equal parts

One cannot exist without the other

Forever caught in time

Wolf Star

The moon rises in the eastern sky draped in orange hues. The night lingers on. The ice moon rises from the horizon, emerging pale yellow and backlit by the constellation of Cancer. Snow falls in the early morning hours. A bright luminous orb cradled by the stars celebrates the conception of the Wolf Star. Nature's cohort is descended from legendary stock. Mystical howls reverberate through the alpine wilderness in melodic affection. Wild and instinctual, the future queen will grow into her cloak of white. This is how her story begins.

Dream

Moe'uhane

Curtain Wall

Adrift, neither asleep nor awake, a cool breeze hints of rain

Billowing dark clouds pregnant with rain, part to a portal into the past

The stronghold's curtain wall, visible through a wispy sky devoid of starlight, holds the promise of a torrential downpour

Battlements with arrow slits revealed in the deluge

Longing slips away in wakefulness

Thunderous rumbling in the squall, as lightning cracks in the firmament drawn to arousal

Recollection slips away like leaves floating on the surface of a river running downstream

Panthera

Fossil footprints pad closer

The air stills as the velvet night nuzzles closer

Curiosity awakens a forgotten relic

A soft blow followed by gentle rake of claws

Deliberate and halting

Seeking to know, like the sun peeking through a storm-darkened sky

The Vision

The warlord returns from conquest

Battle lust rages through his veins

The barbarian enters the ger, his masculine frame
rippling with taut muscles with every purposeful stride.

Searching the smoky ger for his heart's desire

Red silk draperies hide a voluptuous temptress sprawled
on red silk bed coverings and fur pelts

Glossy locks cover snowy peaks and a valley

Waiting longingly for her lord

A welcoming embrace in loving arms

Ebony tresses draped lovingly over a rock-hard frame

His taut muscles beading with glistening sweat,
mingling with battle grim

Essence of man

Straining rhythm

Soft sounds of desire escape the draperies

Strangled cries of ecstasy

Battle cry

Battle lust or passion for his heart's desire

Stolen moments, glimpse of the past

He returns to protect the horde

Love endures the ages

Multihued Rainbow

Lehulehu Anuenue

Blacksmith and Steel

Forge and bellows

Hammer and anvil

Intense heat braved by a master

Strength derived

Opposing forces melded into one

Datsun 510

Rescued from the rubble

Sculpted and buffed

Resurrected old school

Rumbling down the asphalt strip

The sun dancing off her cherried-out chasse

Snapping their necks

Smoke 'em

Enveloped in Darkness

Enveloped in Darkness

Happiness eludes you

Battered and bruised

Reach out, let the shadows lift

Walk into the sunshine to be worshipped and adored

Iron Rose Posse

As the stagecoach approaches an outcropping of rocks
and boulders, thundering hooves pound the ground,
surrounding the coach, surprising the whip

Dust billows in large, muddled clouds

Emerging from the haze gallops Shotgun Sadie astride
her Palomino filly

Lilith Sharp, strapped with her Breecher's Bible,
leaning forward on her steed for speed

The Bandit Queen Quinn seated in her rig, her
Avenging Angel bouncing against the saddle with every
stride of her stallion

Surrounding the coach carrying silver, they draw their
barking irons

The whip pulls hard on the lines to halt the horses as the
shady ladies surround the coach

Swooning for the outlaw lasses on the box, Charlie
halts the mud wagon

In a bag of nails, terrified passengers are relieved of
their finer possessions

The seductive outlaws collect a pretty penny

On the win, the Iron Rose Posse doles a cartwheel to each afeared patron

In a muddle, bustles and bravado vanish into the landscape lickety-split

Milo

A renowned warrior paddles his canoe against the
billowing surf

Greeted by rugged grandeur of Na Pali's emerald-hued
cliffs

His paddle is straight and true

Burying his blade, spray flurries

His prodigious strength is legendary

Beaching his canoe

A solitary sacred tree still rooted lies cleaved in half

Its glossy heart-shaped leaves are tousled by wind and
pelted by rain

Heartwood exposed, creamy and darkened tones

Its widespread branches draped across the seashore like
a fine mat

The sea whispers an arduous task

The mighty man twists the tattered and torn truck

Its light and dark nature battling to balance

Melding distinctive halves

Seashore gem, coveted by royalty

Ovidia

The moon over Delos lights the path to the otherworld

In the shadows of her ancient lands lurk enemies

Deep in thought, her delicate fingers trace through the
coarse fur of the wolf at her side

Her bow chafes her bare shoulder with the weight of a
heavy heart

Cradled in the crook of her arm, she holds a tiny bundle

Primal howls reverberate from the forest interior,
echoing her poignant loss

Mist and fog swirl underfoot as she walks through the
undergrowth, flanked by her loyal companions as she
surveys her realm

War is coming, she can taste it on the cold wind, feel it
in her aching wounds

The first rays of sunlight break the horizon, the battle
awaits

Climbing onto her steed, her battle-worn armor creaks
with her graceful movements

Her stallion paws the moist earth in anticipation and
snorts at the distant threat

The queen glances up at the last stars twinkling in the dawn, a single tear traces her pale cheek for her fallen love

She steels herself, containing a smoldering fire within as she advances to the bitter clash

Her battle commanders and warriors await her arrival on the distant plain

As she approaches her battle-hardened cohorts in the gloom, the stench of the foe is overpowering

One last glance under the covering that cloaks her heir, as she does the babe's little hands fiercely grip her fingers

Relinquishing her precious cargo with a tender kiss, the hidden bundle is secreted away to safety

Turning her attention to the impending doom, outnumbered by her nemesis, their strategic plan must not fail, they must hold back the horde or all is lost

Battle lines are drawn, she thunders into the fray, flanked by her snarling wolves

Metal clashes, swords grind together

The sounds of shrieking steel reverberates through the battlefield

Blood flows in rivulets down her flesh, sweat soaks her armor

Cut off from her arm and surrounded, she will not lose
hope, she must not, too much is at stake

A debilitating blow from behind stuns her as she falls
from her mount

A hazy cloud envelops her body crumpled on the
ground, shrouded by her adversaries

The battle rages on

A babe cries in the distance

Wild Card

Decks are shuffled and dealt

Years pass, seasons change, and lunar cycles wax and
wane

A house of cards is built, magic tricks played, crazy
eights

Never hearts and diamonds, only clubs and spades

Always the jack, never the king

Jack's ever-present poker face

Always the games of bullshit and war played

Where are the suicide kings

Youthful is the jack of diamonds.

His merry laughter sounds like the tinkling bells of
spring

The elegant queen, regal in nature

Does she hold the scepter

Jokers ever-present wit and sarcasm, his laughter heals
the soul

Fifty-two pickup

Cards scattered into the hot breeze warmed by the sun

Discarded deck lying in the grit and grime

Stuck in tumbleweeds

Picked up and dusted off, ready to play again

Go fish

Vixen

Long long ago, Dancer's blessed event was illuminated
by the Christmas star

The tiniest reindeer, Vixen was brought forth

Her dainty grace ringing in merriment and cheer

Watched over with joy and goodwill

Glad-hearted meanderings on a blustery day

Her playful antics left her disorientated, wandering far
from her herd

Fraught with fear, she lets out a throaty call

Circled by golden eagles and stalked by wolverines

Santa's team searches for Vixen, their furred cloven
hooves cleave through the deep snow

Multihued lights dance across the night heavens, Vixen
is nowhere to be found

Through the blinding blizzard, clicking and clacking
resonates

All seems lost in a whirlwind of snow blossoms

Shivering in fright, Vixen cowers under a blanket of
white

Reindeer hooves ring in the distance, like the warm sun seeping through the gloom

Vixen springs forth, meggling through glistening snow drifts

A joyous clamor can be heard as a celebratory reunion occurs

Nuzzling and honking, a glorious sight

Ready to spread Christmas magic throughout the night

Harnesses bedecked with verdant green and silver bells

The littlest reindeer placed in swing

She prances in glee

"Tighten up," musically sounds Santa

"Now dash away," he choruses, "straight ahead," and the sleigh team springs into flight

Tinkling bells can be heard as they disappear into the night

The newest reindeer is a head-turning sight

Stories

Mo'olelo

The Caterpillar

My son found a caterpillar on the caterpillar tree at school. He wanted to bring it home so badly. He said, "Just to spend the night, Mom." He played with the little caterpillar in his little hand, watching him with curious eyes. Touching him ever so gently. When he got tired, he placed the caterpillar in his shoe. He told me, "Don't worry, Mom, he's playing in my shoe. I'm watching him." Driving in stop-and-go traffic, rocking my son to sleep, I looked in the rearview mirror. My son was fast asleep. When we arrived home, lo and behold, the caterpillar was not in his shoe. We scoured the car, looking for the little caterpillar. My son said, "Mom, I didn't mean to lose him." He thought he might have thrown him out with some papers. I reassured him that he was somewhere in the car and he would be all right. I know he never meant to lose him. It's hard being twelve, full of energy, and playing all day at school with your friends. The next day I opened my passenger door to put in my work stuff and what do I see? A tiny chrysalis hanging on the portion of the floor mat that was sticking up. I think of my son and how precious his little caterpillar is to him and how much I love my son. It brightens my heart and makes me smile. I gently remove the fragile chrysalis and place it in a crook that is sheltered from the elements so my son can check on his caterpillar becoming a butterfly.

The Star

I petitioned the gods for a gift. The bestowed a magnif-
icent shining star like no other. It shone brilliantly and
glimmered as I held it in the palm of my hand. Its light
washed over me in a soft tender glow, caressing my flesh
with love. I loved the star so much I thought my heart
would burst with joy. In my need, I held the star too tight.
The star began to seep through the cracks in my fingers
like golden sand spilling to the earth. I released my grip.

As I complete Act I in my journey and begin my new adventure, I would like to leave you with a quote from my son.

"Make this year your best year, where all your dreams come true and you don't wonder."

—Sorin Wilcox

References

Akana-Gooch, Collette L., Kiele Gonzalez, and Sig Zane. *Hānau Ka Ua : Hawaiian Rain Names* . Honolulu, Hawaiʻi: Kamehameha Publishing, 2015. Print.

Pukui, M. K., & Elbert, S. H. (1986). *Hawaiian dictionary: Hawaiian-English, English-Hawaiian*. Honolulu: University of Hawaii Press.

Glossary

'A'ama crab - *grapsus tenuicrustatus*, thin-shelled black
    crab
a hui hou - until we meet again
Aina - earth
Akamai - smart, clever
Akulikuli - indigenous coastal ground cover
An de shealladh - a genetically inherited trait of
    extrasensory perception, Gaelic for "two sights"
Ani - sky
'Āpono - adopt
Buckaloose - to let loose (Hawaiian slang)
Ekolu - three
Ele'ele - black
Hau'puehuehu - snowflake
Hoa aloha - dear friend
Ho'opakele 'ia - rescued
Honu - turtle
Ho'oponopono - to make right, the practice of forgiving
    and healing
'Ilio-holo-i-ka-uaua - Hawaiian monk seal, "dog
    running through rough water"
Inaina - hate
Kauana'oa - *cuscuta sandwichians*, endangered plant
Kāwelu - *eragrostis variabilis*, tufted short-lived
    perennial grass

Keiki - child

Ki'i - image, statue, ancient rock art

Kokua - to help, to give aid or assistance

Kolone popoki - cat colony

Lani - sky

Lilani - rain name, the unexpected rain

Leikoko'ula - rain

Lililehua - the misty rain in Palolo, Oahu

Līpoa - *dictyopteris plagiogramma*, bladelike brown seaweed with a unique aroma

Loulu - *Pritchardia*, palm species

Makai - towards the ocean

Makani - wind

Mano - shark

Ma'o hau hele - *hibiscus brackenridgei*, endemic species

Mauka - toward the mountains

Me ke aloha pumehana - much love, warm greetings, warm regards

Moli - albatross

Moana - ocean

Na keiki pipi - kittens

Nalowale - lost

Nāulu - rain name, sudden shower

Nene - endemic Hawaiian goose

'Ohai - *sesbario tomentosa*, endangered and endemic plant

Ohana - family

Opihi - *cellana exarata*, seaside limpet that lives on the rocks

Pala'a - Hawaiian lace fern

Pikake - *jasminum sambac*, Arabian jasmine
Pohaku - rock, stone
Pakalana - *telosma cordata*, Chinese violet
Pua - flower or blossom
Pulelehua - butterfly
Puahiohio - wind name meaning whirlwind or gust
Puakenikeni - *fagraea berteriana*, "ten-cent flower"
Punumomi - ladybug
Pulelehua - butterfly
Pu'eo - owl
Puu'wai - heart
'Uhane - spirit
'Ula'ula - red
Waikakalaua - a valley on Oahu, Hawaii

Glossary for "Iron Rose Pose"

Barking irons - pistols
Box - stagecoach driver's seat
Cartwheel - silver dollar coin
Charlie - stagecoach driver
Muddle - bring into disorder or confusing state
Mud wagon - style of stagecoach
On the win - winning or making money
Whip - stagecoach driver

Please keep in mind that all Hawaiian words have many meanings. The meanings shared here are the specific translations for the words as they pertain to this particular book's subject matter.

About the Author

Michael Lemes was born and raised on Oahu in Hawai'i. A single mother of two children, Michael became a law enforcement officer, which has been a challenging and rewarding career.

Michael has worked in the customer service industry and as a historical museum interpreter, a fitness and aerial instructor, a personal trainer, and a youth volleyball and soccer coach.

Her passion for animals led her to become a marine mammal trainer. She participated in PhD dissertations and field research in the Hawaiian Islands National Wildlife Refuge, Papahanamokuakea and Kaua'i. She specializes in the rehabilitation of stranded marine mammals.

Her love of athletics led to her competing in various sports, including collegiate volleyball and powerlifting. She has also performed various disciplines of dance.

Guided by her desire to learn, she returned to college as an adult, completing a master's degree.

www.ingramcontent.com/pod-product-compliance
Lightning Source LLC
Chambersburg PA
CBHW030407130626
46549CB00004B/1669